D0571866

The
LITTLE BOOK
of
TALENT

The
LITTLE BOOK
of
TALENT

52
TIPS *for* IMPROVING YOUR SKILLS

Daniel Coyle

BANTAM BOOKS | NEW YORK

Published in the United States by Bantam Books,
an imprint of The Random House Publishing Group,
a division of Random House, Inc., New York.

Bantam Books and the rooster colophon are
registered trademarks of Random House, Inc.

LIBRARY OF CONGRESS
CATALOGING-IN-PUBLICATION DATA

Coyle, Daniel.
The little book of talent : 52 tips for improving skills / Daniel Coyle.
p. cm.
Includes bibliographical references.
ISBN 978-0-345-53025-7
eBook ISBN 978-0-345-53669-3
1. Ability. I. Title.
BF431.C685 2012
153.9—dc23
2012001646

Printed in the United States of America on acid-free paper

www.bantamdell.com

2 4 6 8 9 7 5 3 1

FIRST EDITION

Book design by Casey Hampton

For Jen

We are what we repeatedly do.
Excellence, then, is not an act, but a habit.
— Aristotle

CONTENTS

INTRODUCTION

The Story of the
Little Book

A few years back, on assignment for a magazine, I began visiting talent hotbeds: tiny places that produce large numbers of world-class performers in sports, art, music, business, math, and other disciplines. Places such as:

- A ramshackle Moscow tennis club that had, over the previous three years, produced more Top 20 women players than the entire United States.
- A humble Adirondacks music camp where students accomplish one year's worth of progress in seven weeks.
- A San Mateo, California, inner-city charter school that, in four years, transformed a student population perennially ranked at the bottom of

state math scores into one that scored in the ninety-sixth percentile.

- A Dallas vocal studio that has, over the past decade, developed millions of dollars' worth of pop-music talent.
- A ski academy in Vermont with an enrollment of a hundred that has produced fifty Olympic skiers over the past forty years.

My research also took me to a different sort of hotbed: the laboratories and research centers around the country investigating the new science of talent development. For centuries, people have instinctively assumed that talent is largely innate, a gift given out at birth. But now, thanks to the work of a wide-ranging team of scientists, including Dr. K. Anders Ericsson, Dr. Douglas Fields, and Dr. Robert Bjork, the old beliefs about talent are being overturned. In their place, a new view is being established, one in which talent is determined far less by our genes and far more by our actions: specifically, the combination of intensive practice and motivation that produces brain growth.* My project evolved into a book called *The Talent Code,* which was about how the hot-

---

* Why the brain? Because developing talent is all about growing the brain. "Muscle memory" doesn't really exist, because our muscles simply do what our brains tell them to do. Thus, the new science can be summed up as follows: You want to develop your talent? Build a better brain through intensive practice.

beds succeed by aligning themselves with the brain's natural mechanisms for acquiring skill.

Along the way, however, the journey had an unexpected side effect. Besides being a journalist, I happen to be the father of four, a volunteer baseball coach, and the husband of a hockey-playing wife. As a family, we struggled daily with the usual questions and anxieties that revolve around the process of acquiring and developing skills. How do we help our daughter learn her multiplication tables? How do we tell a genuine talent from a momentary interest? What's the best way to spark motivation? How do we encourage improvement without becoming psycho parents or creating stressed, unhappy kids? As it turned out, visiting these remarkable places was not just a chance for me to be a journalist. It was also a chance to become a better coach and a better dad.

It started when I visited my first talent hotbed, the Spartak Tennis Club in Moscow. On my first morning there, I walked in to see a line of players swinging their racquets in slow motion, without the ball, as a teacher made small, precise adjustments to their form. I noticed the way the teachers routinely mixed age groups. I noticed the riveted, laserlike looks in the younger players' eyes as they watched the older stars, as if they were burning images of perfect forehands and backhands onto their brains. In my brain, a thought began to take shape.

I could really use this stuff back home.

From that point on, whenever I spotted a nugget of advice or a potentially useful method, I jotted it in my notebook and marked the page with an electric-pink Post-it. I scribbled down tips like *Always exaggerate new moves*; *Shrink the practice space;* and (my personal favorite) *Take lots of naps.* Over the course of the year, a forest of pink grew along the edges of my notebook.

The advice turned out to work well—quite well, judging by the swift, steady progress of my kids' violin and piano playing, my wife's hockey skills, and the win-loss record of the Little League team I coached (10-3; the all-star team I coached, which had historically done poorly, nearly advanced to regionals). After *The Talent Code* was published, I began hearing from groups that were using the principles of the book to create talent-development programs of their own—a charter school in Maine, a nursing program in Minnesota, a golf academy in Florida, an SAT-prep course in California, a Division I college basketball team, a software company, military special-ops training organizations, and several professional sports teams. I kept traveling, visiting more talent hotbeds, talking to more master teachers, and adding more pink Post-its. At some point I realized that I needed to organize all this advice and put it in one place.

This book is that place.

What follows is a collection of simple, practical tips

for improving skills, taken directly from the hotbeds I visited and the scientists who research them. The advice is field-tested, scientifically sound, and, most important, concise. Because when it comes down to it, we're all navigating busy, complex lives. Parent or teacher, kid or coach, artist or entrepreneur, we all want to make the most of our time and energy. When it comes to developing our talents, we could use an owner's manual, something to say *Do this, not that*. We could use a master coach that tucks in our pocket. We could use a little book.

How to Use This Book

Let's start with the basics:

1. We all possess talents.
2. We're unsure how to develop those talents to their full potential.

For most of us, the problem revolves around one word: "how." How do we recognize talents in ourselves and in those near us? How do we nurture talent in its early stages? How do we gain the most progress in the least time? How do we choose between different strategies, teachers, and methods?

This book is built on the idea that the best way to develop your talents is to follow the proven techniques of the talent hotbeds. The tips I've collected fall into three natural categories, which form the sections of this book:

1) *Getting Started:* ideas for igniting motivation and creating a blueprint for the skills you want to build.
2) *Improving Skills:* methods and techniques for making the most progress in the least time.
3) *Sustaining Progress:* strategies for overcoming plateaus, keeping motivational fires lit, and building habits for long-term success.

Each section consists of a series of tips. The tips are brief—not because they're oversimplified, but because simplicity is the point. While the underlying neuroscience is fascinating and complex, it all adds up to the basic truth: *Small actions, repeated over time, transform us.* As the master vocal coach Linda Septien put it, "This ain't magic, and it ain't rocket science. It's about working hard, and working smart."

It's also about working in a way that fits our lives. That's why this book is made to be carried—tucked into a pocket, an instrument case, or a sports bag. It's also why it contains blank pages for your notes.*

Whatever talent you set out to build, from golfing to

---

* If you'd like to offer a comment or suggest a new tip to others, go to thetalentcode.com.

learning a new language to playing guitar to managing a startup, be assured of one thing: You are born with the machinery to transform beginners' clumsiness into fast, fluent action. That machinery is not controlled by genes, it's controlled by you. Each day, each practice session, is a step toward a different future. This is a hopeful idea, and the most hopeful thing about it is that it is a fact.

GETTING STARTED

1

Stare, Steal, and
Be Willing to Be Stupid

We are often taught that talent begins with genetic gifts—that the talented are able to effortlessly perform feats the rest of us can only dream about. This is false. Talent begins with brief, powerful encounters that spark motivation by linking your identity to a high-performing person or group. This is called ignition, and it consists of a tiny, world-shifting thought lighting up your unconscious mind: *I could be them.*

This first section is about creating the ignition moment, and about channeling its energy in the most constructive way. The tips cover several areas—mind-set, how to design your practice for the skills you want to build, and how to improve your learning by stealing effectively from top performers—but they share the same goal: to create the spark, and to use the fuel for deep practice.

TIP #1
STARE AT WHO YOU WANT TO BECOME

If you were to visit a dozen talent hotbeds tomorrow, you would be struck by how much time the learners spend observing top performers. When I say "observing," I'm not talking about passively watching. I'm talking about staring—the kind of raw, unblinking, intensely absorbed gazes you see in hungry cats or newborn babies.

We each live with a "windshield" of people in front of us; one of the keys to igniting your motivation is to fill your windshield with vivid images of your future self, and to stare at them every day. Studies show that even a brief connection with a role model can vastly increase unconscious motivation. For example, being told that you share a birthday with a mathematician can improve the amount of effort you're willing to put into difficult math tasks by 62 percent.

Many talent hotbeds are fueled by the windshield

phenomenon. In 1997, there were no South Korean golfers on the Ladies Professional Golf Association (LPGA) Tour. Today there are more than forty, winning one-third of all events. What happened? One golfer succeeded (Se Ri Pak, who won two major tournaments in 1998), and, through her, hundreds of South Korean girls were ignited by a new vision of their future selves. As the South Korean golfer Christina Kim put it, "You say to yourself, 'If she can do it, why can't I?'"

Windshields apply equally well to adults. The 5th Special Forces Group of the Green Berets recently started a leadership-training program in which soldiers spent several weeks in the executive offices of General Electric. The soldiers went to the office each morning and accompanied the execs throughout their workday, with no responsibilities other than to simply observe. And when the soldiers returned to their unit, the commanders noticed a significant boost in performance, communication, and leadership. "It was definitely a success," said Lieutenant Colonel Dean Franks, the 5th Group's battalion commander. "We're planning to do a lot more of this in the future."

Think of your windshield as an energy source for your brain. Use pictures (the walls of many talent hotbeds are cluttered with photos and posters of their stars) or, better, video. One idea: Bookmark a few YouTube videos, and watch them before you practice, or at night before you go to bed.

TIP #2

SPEND FIFTEEN MINUTES A DAY ENGRAVING
THE SKILL ON YOUR BRAIN

What's the best way to begin to learn a new skill? Is it by listening to a teacher's explanation? Reading an instructional book? Just leaping in and trying it out? Many hotbeds use an approach I call the engraving method. Basically, they watch the skill being performed, closely and with great intensity, over and over, until they build a high-definition mental blueprint.

A few years back, for the TV show *60 Minutes,* the tennis teacher and author Timothy Gallwey assembled a group of middle-aged people who'd never played tennis before. He gave them a brief test of ability, and then selected the woman who showed the least potential. Then, *without uttering a word,* Gallwey began to hit a forehand while the woman watched. He directed her attention to his feet, his grip, and the rhythm of the stroke. The woman watched intently, then began to emulate his moves. Within twenty minutes, she was hitting a shockingly decent forehand.

Another example of engraving, which involves the ears instead of the eyes, is the Suzuki method for learning music. Each day, separate from their lessons, Suzuki students listen to a menu of songs, beginning with "Twinkle, Twinkle, Little Star" and progressing by degrees to more complex tunes. Hearing the songs over and over (and over), engraves the songs in the students's brains. The "listening practice" builds a strong, detailed mental map, a series of points from which the success or failure of each following attempt can be measured.

The key to effective engraving is to create an intense connection: to watch and listen so closely that you can imagine the *feeling* of performing the skill. For physical skills, project yourself inside the performer's body. Become aware of the movement, the rhythm; try to feel the interior shape of the moves. For mental skills, simulate the skill by re-creating the expert's decision patterns. Chess players achieve this by replaying classic games, move by move; public speakers do it by regiving great speeches complete with original inflections; musicians cover their favorite songs; some writers I know achieve this effect by retyping passages verbatim from great works. (It sounds kind of Zen, but it works.)

TIP #3
STEAL WITHOUT APOLOGY

We are often told that talented people acquire their skill by following their "natural instincts." This sounds nice, but in fact it is baloney. All improvement is about absorbing and applying new information, and the best source of information is top performers. So steal it.

Stealing has a long tradition in art, sports, and design, where it often goes by the name of "influence." The young Steve Jobs stole the idea for the computer mouse and drop-down menus from the Xerox Palo Alto Research Center. The young Beatles stole the high "wooooo" sounds in "She Loves You," "From Me to You," and "Twist and Shout" from their idol Little Richard. The young Babe Ruth based his swing on the mighty uppercut of his hero, Shoeless Joe Jackson. As Pablo Picasso (no slouch at theft himself) put it, "Good artists borrow. Great artists steal."

Linda Septien, founder of the Septien School of

Contemporary Music, a hotbed near Dallas that has produced millions of dollars in pop-music talent (including Demi Lovato, Ryan Cabrera, and Jessica Simpson), tells her students, "Sweetheart, you gotta steal like crazy. Look at every single performer better than you and see what they've got that you can use. Then make it your own." Septien follows her own advice, having accumulated fourteen three-ring notebooks' worth of ideas stolen from top performers. In plastic sleeves inside the binders, in some cases scribbled on cocktail napkins, reside tips on everything from how to hit a high note to how to deal with a rowdy crowd (a joke works best).

Stealing helps shed light on some mysterious patterns of talent—for instance, why the younger members of musical families so often are also the most talented. (A partial list: The Bee Gees's younger brother, Andy Gibb; Michael Jackson; the youngest Jonas Brother, Nick. Not to mention Mozart, J. S. Bach, and Yo-Yo Ma, all babies of their families.) The difference can be explained partly by the windshield phenomenon (see Tip #1) and partly by theft. As they grow up, the younger kids have more access to good information. They have far more opportunity to watch their older siblings perform, to mimic, to see what works and what doesn't. In other words, to steal.

When you steal, focus on specifics, not general impressions. Capture concrete facts: the angle of a golfer's left elbow at the top of the backswing; the curve of a surgeon's wrist; the precise shape and tension of a singer's lips as he hits that high note; the exact length of time a comedian pauses before delivering the punch line. Ask yourself:

- What, exactly, are the critical moves here?
- How do they perform those moves differently than I do?

TIP #4
BUY A NOTEBOOK

A high percentage of top performers keeps some form of daily performance journal. Tennis champion Serena Williams and former World Series MVP Curt Schilling use notebooks; the rapper Eminem and the choreographer Twyla Tharp use shoeboxes, which they fill with ideas written on scrap paper. What matters is not the precise form. What matters is that you write stuff down and reflect on it. *Results from today. Ideas for tomorrow. Goals for next week.* A notebook works like a map: It creates clarity.

TIP #5
BE WILLING TO BE STUPID

Teammates of the hockey star Wayne Gretzky would occasionally witness a strange sight: Gretzky falling while he skated through solitary drills on the ice. While the spectacle of the planet's greatest hockey player toppling over like a grade-schooler might seem surprising, it actually makes perfect sense. As skilled as he was, Gretzky was determined to improve, to push the boundaries of the possible. The only way that happens is to build new connections in the brain—which means reaching, failing, and, yes, looking stupid.

Feeling stupid is no fun. But being willing to be stupid—in other words, being willing to risk the emotional pain of making mistakes—is absolutely essential, because reaching, failing, and reaching again is the way your brain grows and forms new connections. When it comes to developing talent, remember, mistakes are not really mistakes—they are the guideposts you use to get better.

One way some places encourage "productive mistakes" is to establish rules that encourage people to make reaches that might otherwise feel strange and risky—in effect, nudging them into the sweet spot at the edge of their ability (see Tip #13). For example, students at the Meadowmount School of Music often practice according to an informal rule: If a passerby can recognize a song, it's being played too fast. The point of this super-exaggerated slowness (which produces songs that resemble those of humpback whales) is to reveal small mistakes that might have gone undetected, and thus create more high-quality reaches.

Businesses do it too. Google offers "20-percent time": Engineers are given 20 percent of their work time to spend on private, nonapproved projects they are passionate about, and thus ones for which they are more likely to take risks. I've encountered numerous organizations that have employees sign a "contract" affirming that they will take risks and make mistakes. Living-Social, the Washington, D.C., e-commerce company, has a rule of thumb for employees: Once a week, you should make a decision at work that scares you.

Whatever the strategy, the goal is always the same: to encourage reaching, and to reinterpret mistakes so that they're not verdicts, but the information you use to navigate to the correct move.

TIP #6

CHOOSE SPARTAN OVER LUXURIOUS

We love comfort. We love state-of-the-art practice facili-
ties, oak-paneled corner offices, spotless locker rooms,
and fluffy towels. Which is a shame, because luxury is a
motivational narcotic: It signals our unconscious minds
to give less effort. It whispers, *Relax, you've made it.*

The talent hotbeds are not luxurious. In fact, they
are so much the opposite that they are sometimes called
chicken-wire Harvards. Top music camps—especially
ones that can afford better—consist mainly of rundown
cabins. The North Baltimore Aquatic Club, which
produced Michael Phelps and four other Olympic
medalists, could pass for an underfunded YMCA. The
world's highest-performing schools—those in Finland
and South Korea, which perennially score at the top of
the Program for International Student Assessment
rankings—feature austere classrooms that look as if
they haven't changed since the 1950s.

The point of this tip is not moral; it's neural. Simple, humble spaces help focus attention on the deep-practice task at hand: reaching and repeating and struggling. When given the choice between luxurious and spartan, choose spartan. Your unconscious mind will thank you.

TIP #7
BEFORE YOU START, FIGURE OUT IF IT'S
A HARD SKILL OR A SOFT SKILL

The first step toward building a skill is to figure out exactly what type of skill you're building. Every skill falls into one of two categories: hard skills and soft skills.

HARD, HIGH-PRECISION SKILLS are actions that are performed as correctly and consistently as possible, every time. They are skills that have one path to an ideal result; skills that you could imagine being performed by a reliable robot. Hard skills are about *repeatable precision,* and tend to be found in specialized pursuits, particularly physical ones. Some examples:

- a golfer swinging a club, a tennis player serving, or any precise, repeating athletic move;
- a child performing basic math (for example, addition or the multiplication tables);

- a violinist playing a specific chord;
- a basketball player shooting a free throw;
- a young reader translating letter shapes into sounds and words;
- a worker on an assembly line, attaching a part.

Here, your goal is to build a skill that functions like a Swiss watch—reliable, exact, and performed the same way every time, automatically, without fail. Hard skills are about ABC: Always Being Consistent.

SOFT, HIGH-FLEXIBILITY SKILLS, on the other hand, are those that have many paths to a good result, not just one. These skills aren't about doing the same thing perfectly every time, but rather about being agile and interactive; about instantly recognizing patterns as they unfold and making smart, timely choices. Soft skills tend to be found in broader, less-specialized pursuits, especially those that involve communication, such as:

- a soccer player sensing a weakness in the defense and deciding to attack;
- a stock trader spotting a hidden opportunity amid a chaotic trading day;
- a novelist instinctively shaping the twists of a complicated plot;

- a singer subtly interpreting the music to highlight emotion;
- a police officer on a late-night patrol, assessing potential danger;
- a CEO "reading a room" in a tense meeting or negotiation.

With these skills, we are not trying for Swiss-watch precision, but rather for the ability to quickly recognize a pattern or possibility, and to work past a complex set of obstacles. Soft skills are about the three Rs: Reading, Recognizing, and Reacting.

The point of this tip is that hard skills and soft skills are different (literally, they use different structures of circuits in your brain), and thus are developed through different methods of deep practice.

Begin by asking yourself which of these skills need to be absolutely 100-percent consistent every single time. Which need to be executed with machinelike precision? These are the hard skills.

Then ask yourself, which skills need to be flexible, and variable, and depend on the situation? Which depend on instantly recognizing patterns and selecting one optimal choice? These are the soft skills.

If you aren't sure if the skill is hard or soft, here's a quick litmus test: Is a teacher or coach usually involved in the early stages? If the answer is yes, then it's likely a hard skill. If it's no, then it's a soft skill. Violinists and figure skaters tend to have teachers; CEOs and stand-up comics don't. The following three tips take this idea further, explaining the methods of deep practice that work best to develop each type of skill.

TIP #8

TO BUILD HARD SKILLS,
WORK LIKE A CAREFUL CARPENTER

To develop reliable hard skills, you need to connect the right wires in your brain. In this, it helps to be careful, slow, and keenly attuned to errors. To work like a careful carpenter.

A good example of hard-skill carpentry is found in the Suzuki music instruction method. Suzuki students begin by spending several lessons simply learning to hold the bow and the violin with the right finger curve and pressure, the right stance, the right posture. Using rhyme and repetition, they learn to move the bow (without the violin) "up like a rocket, down like the rain, back and forth like a choo-choo train." Each fundamental, no matter how humble-seeming, is introduced as a precise skill of huge importance (which, of course, it really is), taught via a series of vivid images, and worked on over and over until it is mastered. The vital pieces are built, rep by careful rep.

Another example can be found on a worn piece of paper inside the wallet of Tom Brady, the three-time Super Bowl–winning quarterback of the New England Patriots. On that paper is a handwritten list of fundamental keys to throwing technique. All of them are simple (example: "Throw down the hall"), and all of them connect to the drills Brady's been doing with his personal coach Tom Martinez since he was fourteen years old. In fact, until Martinez died in 2012, Brady visited his coach once or twice a year for a tune-up—or, to put it more accurately, a repaving of Brady's neural highways to make sure they were still running smoothly.

Precision especially matters early on, because the first reps establish the pathways for the future. Neurologists call this the "sled on a snowy hill" phenomenon. The first repetitions are like the first sled tracks on fresh snow: On subsequent tries, your sled will tend to follow those grooves. "Our brains are good at building connections," says Dr. George Bartzokis, a neurologist at UCLA. "They're not so good at unbuilding them."

When you learn hard skills, be precise and measured. Go slowly. Make one simple move at a time, repeating and perfecting it before you move on. Pay attention to errors, and fix them, particularly at the start. Learning fundamentals only *seems* boring—in fact, it's the key moment of investment. If you build the right pathway now, you'll save yourself a lot of time and trouble down the line.

TIP #9
TO BUILD SOFT SKILLS,
PLAY LIKE A SKATEBOARDER

Soft skills catch our eye because they are beautiful: Picture the soccer star Lionel Messi improvising his way to a brilliant goal, or Jimi Hendrix blazing through a guitar solo, or Jon Stewart riffing through a comic monologue. These talents appear utterly magical and unique. In fact they are the result of super-fast brain software recognizing patterns and responding in just the right way.

While hard skills are best put together with measured precision (see Tip #8), soft skills are built by playing and exploring inside challenging, ever-changing environments. These are places where you encounter different obstacles and respond to them over and over, building the network of sensitive wiring you need to read, recognize, and react. In other words, to build soft skills you should behave less like a careful carpenter and more like a skateboarder in a skateboard park: aggressive, curious, and experimental, always seeking new ways to challenge yourself.

Brazil, home of many of the world's most skilled soccer players, develops its players through a unique game called *futebol de salão* ("soccer in the room"). This insanely fast, tightly compressed five-on-five version of the game—played on a field the size of a basketball court—creates 600 percent more touches, demands instant pattern recognition and, in the words of Emilio Miranda, a professor of soccer at the University of São Paulo, serves as Brazil's "laboratory of improvisation."

Chicago's Second City, the comedy troupe that has served as a training ground for some of America's most successful comedians (alumni include Bill Murray, John Belushi, John Candy, Steve Carell, Stephen Colbert, and Tina Fey, among others) accomplishes this by providing a rich, competitive, endlessly varied space in which to practice improvisation, sketch comedy, and stand-up. (For a good example of how profoundly this can improve skills, go to YouTube and look up Tina Fey's Second City work from the '90s. On second thought, don't.) Even the most creative skills—*especially* the most creative skills—require long periods of clumsiness.

The Brontë sisters, three of whom became world-class novelists, built their talents by writing thousands of pages of stories in tiny homemade books when they were children. The early Brontë stories, like Fey's early improv work, aren't very good—and that's precisely the point. They became skilled by performing thousands of intensive reaches and reps in an endlessly challenging, variable, engaging space.

When you practice a soft skill, focus on making a high number of varied reps, and on getting clear feedback. Don't worry too much about making errors—the important thing is to explore. Soft skills are often more fun to practice, but they're also tougher because they demand that you coach yourself. After each session ask yourself, What worked? What didn't? And why?

TIP #10
HONOR THE HARD SKILLS

As you probably recognize, most talents are not exclusively hard skills or soft skills, but rather a combination of the two. For example, think of a violinist's precise finger placement to play a series of notes (a hard skill) and her ability to interpret the emotion of a song (a soft skill). Or a quarterback's ability to deliver an accurate spiral (a hard skill) and his ability to swiftly read a defense (a soft skill).

The point of this tip is simple: Prioritize the hard skills because in the long run they're more important to your talent. At Spartak, the Moscow tennis club, there is a rule that young players must wait years before entering competitive tournaments. "Technique is everything," said a coach, Larisa Preobrazhenskaya. "If you begin playing without technique it is big mistake."

You might be surprised to learn that many top performers place great importance on practicing the same skills they practiced as beginners. The cellist Yo-Yo Ma spends the first minutes of every practice playing single notes on his cello. The NFL quarterback Peyton Manning spends the first segment of every practice doing basic footwork drills—the kind they teach twelve-year-olds. These performers don't say to themselves, "Hey, I'm one of the most talented people in the world—shouldn't I be doing something more challenging?" They resist the temptation of complexity and work on the task of honing and maintaining their hard skills, because those form—quite literally—the foundation of everything else.

One way to keep this idea in mind is to picture your talent as a big oak tree—a massive, thick trunk of hard skills with a towering canopy of flexible soft skills up above. First build the trunk. Then work on the branches.

TIP #11
DON'T FALL FOR THE PRODIGY MYTH

Most of us grow up being taught that talent is an inheritance, like brown hair or blue eyes. Therefore, we presume that the surest sign of talent is early, instant, effortless success, i.e., being a prodigy. In fact, a well-established body of research shows that that assumption is false. Early success turns out to be a weak predictor of long-term success.

Many top performers are overlooked early on, then grow quietly into stars. This list includes Michael Jordan (cut from his high school varsity team as a sophomore), Charles Darwin (considered slow and ordinary by teachers), Walt Disney (fired from an early job because he "lacked imagination"), Albert Einstein, Louis Pasteur, Paul Gauguin, Thomas Edison, Leo Tolstoy, Fred Astaire, Winston Churchill, Lucille Ball, and so on. One theory, put forth by Dr. Carol Dweck of Stanford University, is that the praise and attention prodigies receive lead them to instinctively protect their "magical" status by taking fewer risks, which eventually slows their learning.

The talent hotbeds are not built on identifying talent, but on constructing it, day by day. They are not overly impressed by precociousness and do not pretend to know who will succeed. While I was visiting the U.S. Olympic Training Center at Colorado Springs, I asked a roomful of fifty experienced coaches this question: Could they accurately assess a top fifteen-year-old's chances of winning a medal in Games two years from then? Only one coach raised his hand.*

Anson Dorrance, the head coach of the University of North Carolina women's soccer team, which he has led to twenty-one national championship wins, sums this up nicely. "One of the most unfortunate things I see when identifying youth players is the girl who is told over the years how great she is. By the time she's a high school freshman, she starts to believe it. By her senior year, she's fizzled out. Then there's her counterpart: a girl waiting in the wings, who quietly and with determination decides she's going to make something of herself. Invariably, this humble, hardworking girl is the one who becomes the real player."

If you have early success, do your best to ignore the

* Unsurprisingly, it was the gymnastics coach, who works in a sport where athletes peak early and body type plays a dominant role.

praise and keep pushing yourself to the edges of your ability, where improvement happens. If you don't have early success, don't quit. Instead, treat your early efforts as experiments, not as verdicts. Remember, this is a marathon, not a sprint.

TIP #12
FIVE WAYS TO PICK A HIGH-QUALITY TEACHER OR COACH

Great teachers, coaches, and mentors, like any rare species, can be identified by a few characteristic traits. The following rules are designed to help you sort through the candidates and make the best choice for yourself.

1) Avoid Someone Who Reminds You of a Courteous Waiter

This species of teacher/coach/mentor is increasingly abundant in our world: one who focuses his efforts on keeping you comfortable and happy, on making things go smoothly, with a minimum of effort. This is the kind of person who covers a lot of material in a short time, smiles a lot, and says things like, "Don't worry, no problem, we can take care of that later." This is a good person to have as your waiter in a restaurant, but a terrible person to have as your teacher, coach, or mentor.

2) Seek Someone Who Scares You a Little

In contrast to encounters with courteous waiters, encounters with great teachers/coaches/mentors tend to be filled with unfamiliar emotion: feelings of respect, admiration, and, often, a shiver of fear. This is a good sign. Look for someone who:

Watches you closely: He is interested in figuring you out—what you want, where you're coming from, what motivates you.

Is action-oriented: She often won't want to spend a lot of time chatting—instead, she'll want to jump into a few activities immediately, so she can get a feel for you and vice versa.

Is honest, sometimes unnervingly so: He will tell you the truth about your performance in clear language. This stings at first. But you'll come to see that it's not personal—it's the information you can use to get better.

It's worth noting that the word "coach" originally came from *kocsi,* the Hungarian word for "carriage." You're not looking for a buddy or a parent figure. You're looking for someone solid, someone you trust, someone with whom you take a journey.

3) Seek Someone Who Gives Short, Clear Directions

Most great teachers/coaches/mentors do not give long-winded speeches. They do not give sermons or long lectures. Instead, they give short, unmistakably clear directions; they guide you to a target.

John Wooden, the UCLA basketball coach who is widely considered one of the greatest teachers of all time, was once the subject of a yearlong study that captured everything he said to his team. Wooden didn't give long speeches; in fact, his average utterance lasted only four seconds. This underlines a large truth: Teaching is not an eloquence contest; it is about creating a connection and delivering useful information.

4) Seek Someone Who Loves Teaching Fundamentals

Great teachers will often spend entire practice sessions on one seemingly small fundamental—for example, the way you grip a golf club, or the way you pluck a single note on a guitar. This might seem strange, but it reflects their understanding of a vital reality: These fundamentals are the core of your skills (see Tip #10). The more advanced you are, the more crucial they become.

5) Other Things Being Equal, Pick the Older Person

Teaching is like any other talent: It takes time to grow. This is why so many hotbeds are led by people in their sixties and seventies. Great teachers are first and foremost learners, who improve their skills with each passing year. That's not to say there aren't any good teachers under thirty—there are. Nor is it to say that every coach with gray hair is a genius—they're not. But other things being equal, go with someone older.

IMPROVING SKILLS

Find the Sweet Spot,
Then Reach

If I had to sum up the difference between people in the talent hotbeds and people everywhere else in one sentence, it would be this:

People in the hotbeds have a different relationship with practicing.

Many of us view practice as necessary drudgery, the equivalent of being forced to eat your vegetables, far less important or interesting than the big game or the big performance. But in the talent hotbeds I visited, practice *was* the big game, the center of their world, the main focus of their daily lives. This approach succeeds because over time, practice is transformative, if it's the right kind of practice. Deep practice.

The key to deep practice is to reach. This means to stretch yourself slightly beyond your current ability, spending time in the zone of difficulty called the sweet spot. It means embracing the power of repetition, so the action becomes fast and automatic. It means creating a practice space that enables you to reach and repeat, stay engaged, and improve your skills over time.

The previous section was about getting ready. This section is about action: simple strategies and techniques to direct you toward deep practice and nudge you away from the unproductive swamp of shallow practice.

TIP #13
FIND THE SWEET SPOT

There is a place, right on the edge of your ability, where you learn best and fastest. It's called the sweet spot. Here's how to find it.

[Comfort Zone]

Sensations: Ease, effortlessness. You're working, but not reaching or struggling.

Percentage of Successful Attempts: 80 percent and above.

[Sweet Spot]

Sensations: Frustration, difficulty, alertness to errors. You're fully engaged in an intense struggle—as if you're stretching with all your might for a nearly unreachable goal, brushing it with your fingertips, then reaching again.

Percentage of Successful Attempts: 50–80 percent.

[Survival Zone]

Sensations: Confusion, desperation. You're overmatched: scrambling, thrashing, and guessing. You guess right sometimes, but it's mostly luck.

Percentage of Successful Attempts: Below 50 percent.

To understand the importance of the sweet spot, consider Clarissa, a freckle-faced thirteen-year-old clarinet player who was part of a study by two Australian music psychologists named Gary McPherson and James Renwick. Clarissa was an average musician, in every sense of the word—average ability, average practice habits, average motivation. But one morning, a remarkable thing happened: Clarissa accomplished a month's worth of practice in five minutes.

Here's what it looked like: Clarissa played a few notes. Then she made a mistake and immediately froze, as if the clarinet were electrified. She peered closely at the sheet music, reading the notes. She hummed the notes to herself. She fingered the keys in a fast, silent rehearsal. Then she started again, got a bit farther, made another mistake, stopped again, and went back to the start. In this fashion, working instinctively, she learned the song. McPherson calculated that Clarissa learned more in that span of five minutes than she would have learned in an entire month practicing her normal way, in which she played songs straight through, ignoring any mistakes.

Why? Picture the wires of Clarissa's brain during those five minutes. Each time she made a mistake, she was 1) sensing it and 2) fixing it, welding the right connection in her brain. Each time she repeated the passage, she was strengthening those connections and linking them together. She was not just practicing. She was building her brain. She was in the sweet spot.

Locating your sweet spot requires some creativity. For instance, some golfers work on their swings underwater (which slows them down, so they can sense and fix their mistakes). Some musicians play songs backward (which helps them better sense the relationship between the notes). These are different methods, but the underlying pattern is the same: Seek out ways to stretch yourself. Play on the edges of your competence. As Albert Einstein said, "One must develop an instinct for what one can just barely achieve through one's greatest efforts."

The key word is "barely." Ask yourself: If you tried your absolute hardest, what could you *almost* do? Mark the boundary of your current ability, and aim a little beyond it. That's your spot.

TIP #14
TAKE OFF YOUR WATCH

Deep practice is not measured in minutes or hours, but in the number of high-quality reaches and repetitions you make—basically, how many new connections you form in your brain.

Instead of counting minutes or hours, count reaches and reps. Instead of saying, "I'm going to practice piano for twenty minutes," tell yourself, "I'm going to do five intensive reps of that new song." Instead of planning to hit golf balls for an hour, plan to make twenty-five quality swings with each club. Instead of reading over that textbook for an hour, make flash cards and grade yourself on your efforts. Ignore the clock and get to the sweet spot, even if it's only for a few minutes, and measure your progress by what counts: reaches and reps.

TIP #15
BREAK EVERY MOVE DOWN INTO CHUNKS

From the time we're small, we hear this good advice from our parents and teachers: *Take it a little bit at a time.* This advice works because it accurately reflects the way our brains learn. Every skill is built out of smaller pieces—what scientists call chunks.

Chunks are to skill what letters of the alphabet are to language. Alone, each is nearly useless, but when combined into bigger chunks (words), and when those chunks are combined into still bigger things (sentences, paragraphs), they can build something complex and beautiful.

To begin chunking, first engrave the blueprint of the skill on your mind (see Tip #2). Then ask yourself:

1) What is the smallest single element of this skill that I can master?
2) What other chunks link to that chunk?

Practice one chunk by itself until you've mastered it—then connect more chunks, one by one, exactly as you would combine letters to form a word. Then combine *those* chunks into still bigger chunks. And so on.

Musicians at Meadowmount cut apart musical scores with scissors and put the pieces in a hat, then pull each section out at random. Then, after the chunks are learned separately, they start combining them in the correct order, like so many puzzle pieces. "It works because the students aren't just playing the music on autopilot—they're thinking," says one of the school's violin instructors, Skye Carman.

No matter what skill you set out to learn, the pattern is always the same: See the whole thing. Break it down to its simplest elements. Put it back together. Repeat.

TIP #16

EACH DAY, TRY TO BUILD
ONE PERFECT CHUNK

In our busy lives, it's sometimes tempting to regard merely practicing as a success. We complete the appointed hour and sigh victoriously—mission accomplished! But the real goal isn't practice; it's progress. As John Wooden put it, "Never mistake mere activity for accomplishment."

One useful method is to set a daily SAP: smallest achievable perfection. In this technique, you pick a single chunk that you can perfect—not just improve, not just "work on," but get 100 percent consistently correct. For example, a tennis player might choose the service toss; a salesperson might choose the twenty-second pitch he'll make to an important client. The point is to take the time to aim at a small, defined target, and then put all your effort toward hitting it.

After all, you aren't built to be transformed in a single day. You are built to improve little by little, connection by connection, rep by rep. As Wooden also said, "Don't look for the big, quick improvement. Seek the small improvement one day at a time. That's the only way it happens—and when it happens, it lasts."

TIP #17
EMBRACE STRUGGLE

At all of the talent hotbeds, from Moscow to Dallas to Brazil to New York, I saw the same facial expression: eyes narrow, jaw tight, nostrils flared, the face of someone intently reaching for something, falling short, and reaching again. This is not a coincidence. Deep practice has a telltale emotional flavor, a feeling that can be summed up in one word: "struggle."

Most of us instinctively avoid struggle, because it's uncomfortable. It feels like failure. However, when it comes to developing your talent, struggle isn't an option—it's a biological necessity. This might sound strange, but it's the way evolution has built us. The struggle and frustration you feel at the edges of your abilities—that uncomfortable burn of "almost, almost"—is the sensation of constructing new neural connections, a phenomenon that the UCLA psychologist Robert Bjork calls "desirable difficulty." Your brain works just like your muscles: no pain, no gain.

TIP #18

CHOOSE FIVE MINUTES A DAY OVER
AN HOUR A WEEK

With deep practice, small daily practice "snacks" are more effective than once-a-week practice binges. The reason has to do with the way our brains grow—incrementally, a little each day, even as we sleep. Daily practice, even for five minutes, nourishes this process, while more occasional practice forces your brain to play catch-up. Or, as the music-education pioneer Shinichi Suzuki puts it, "Practice on the days that you eat."

How short can these segments be? Hans Jensen, a cello teacher at Northwestern University, provided an example when he taught a time-strapped medical student who desired to practice only *two* minutes a day. Working systematically, they broke a piece into its component passages, tackling the toughest ones first. The student was able to successfully learn a complex étude in six weeks. "We were shocked at how well it went," Jensen said. "The key was total focus and being ruthless about noticing and fixing every tiny mistake from the start."

The other advantage of practicing daily is that it becomes a habit. The act of practicing—making time to do it, doing it well—can be thought of as a skill in itself, perhaps the most important skill of all. Give it time. According to research, establishing a new habit takes about thirty days.

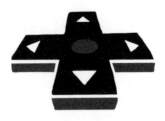

TIP #19
DON'T DO "DRILLS." INSTEAD,
PLAY SMALL, ADDICTIVE GAMES

This tip is about the way you think about your practice.
The term "drill" evokes a sense of drudgery and mean-
inglessness. It's mechanical, repetitive, and boring—as
the saying goes, drill and kill. Games, on the other
hand, are precisely the opposite. They mean fun, con-
nectedness, and passion. And because of that, skills improve faster when they're looked at this way.

Dig into the biography of any world-class performer
and you'll uncover a story about a small, addictive game.
Whether it's the young golfer Rory McIlroy chipping
golf balls into the family dryer, or Warren Buffett as a
child going door-to-door selling chewing gum and trying to figure out what flavor sold best, or Keith Rich-
ards in the early days of the Rolling Stones trying to
decode a riff on an old blues record, what they have in

common is a juicy, addictive sense of involvement, fun, and excitement.

Good coaches share a knack for transforming the most mundane activities—*especially* the most mundane activities—into games. The governing principle is this: If it can be counted, it can be turned into a game. For example, playing a series of guitar chords as a drill is boring. But if you count the number of times you do it perfectly and give yourself a point for each perfect chord, it can become a game. Track your progress, and see how many points you score over a week. The following week, try to score more.

TIP #20
PRACTICE ALONE

Solo practice works because it's the best way to 1) seek out the sweet spot at the edge of your ability, and 2) develop discipline, because it doesn't depend on others. A classic study of musicians compared world-class performers with top amateurs. The researchers found that the two groups were similar in every practice variable except one: The world-class performers spent *five times* as many hours practicing alone.

As the North Carolina women's soccer coach Anson Dorrance said, "The vision of a champion is someone who is bent over, drenched in sweat, at the point of exhaustion, when no one else is watching."

TIP #21
THINK IN IMAGES

Which of the following instructions is easier to remember?

- Take the tennis racket back in a straight horizontal line.
- Take the tennis racket back as if you were sweeping dishes off a coffee table.

- Sing the phrase more quietly at the end.
- Sing the phrase like a balloon running out of air.

- Touch the strings as lightly as possible.
- Touch the strings as if they were burning hot.

- Trap the soccer ball gently.
- Let the ball kiss your foot.

The images are far easier to grasp, recall, and per-form. This is because your brain spent millions of years evolving to register images more vividly and memorably than abstract ideas. (After all, in prehistoric days, no one ever had to worry about getting eaten by a hungry idea. But they did have to worry about lions.)

Whenever possible, create a vivid image for each chunk you want to learn. The images don't have to be elaborate, just easy to see and feel.

TIP #22

PAY ATTENTION IMMEDIATELY AFTER
YOU MAKE A MISTAKE

Most of us are allergic to mistakes. When we make one, our every instinct urges us to look away, ignore it, and pretend it didn't happen. This is not good, because as we've seen, mistakes are our guideposts for improvement. Brain-scan studies reveal a vital instant, 0.25 seconds after a mistake is made, in which people do one of two things—they look hard at the mistake or they ignore it. People who pay deeper attention to an error learn significantly more than those who ignore it.

Develop the habit of attending to your errors right away. Don't wince, don't close your eyes; look straight at them and see what really happened, and ask yourself what you can do next to improve. Take mistakes seriously, but never personally.

TIP #23
VISUALIZE THE WIRES OF
YOUR BRAIN FORMING NEW CONNECTIONS

When you go to the sweet spot on the edge of your ability and reach beyond it, you are forming and strengthening new connections in your brain. Mistakes aren't really mistakes, then—they're the information you use to build the right links. The more you pay attention to mistakes and fix them, the more of the *right* connections you'll be building inside your brain. Visualizing this process as it happens helps you reinterpret mistakes as what they actually are: tools for building skill.

TIP #24
VISUALIZE THE WIRES OF
YOUR BRAIN GETTING FASTER

Every time you practice deeply—the wires of your brain get faster. Over time, signal speeds increase to 200 mph from 2 mph. When you practice, it's useful and motivating to visualize the pathways of your brain being transformed from simple copper wires to high-speed broadband, because that's what's really happening. (For more on this process, see the Appendix on page 117.)

TIP #25
SHRINK THE SPACE

Smaller practice spaces can deepen practice when they are used to increase the number and intensity of the reps and clarify the goal. A good example is used by FC Barcelona, widely considered the world's best soccer team. The method is simple: one room slightly bigger than a bathroom, two players, and one ball—whoever can keep the ball from the other player longest wins. This little game isolates and compresses a vital skill—ball control—by creating a series of urgent, struggle-filled crises to which the players respond and thus improve. "It looks very crazy," says a former Barcelona academy coach named Rodolfo Borrell. "But it works." I used a version of this idea to teach my Little League baseball team defensive situations (which player covers which base), and we had several productive sessions in a space no bigger than a living room. My favorite part? Not having to shout across the field.

This tip does not apply to just physical space. Poets and writers shrink the field by using restrictive meters to force themselves into a small creative form—such as with haiku and micro-writing exercises. Comedy writers use the 140-character arena of Twitter as a space to hone their skills. Businesses can also benefit from compression: Toyota trains new employees by shrinking the assembly line into a single room filled with toy-sized replicas of its equipment. The company has found that this mini-training is more effective than training on the actual production line.

Ask yourself: What's the minimum space needed to make these reaches and reps? Where is extra space hindering fast and easy communication?

TIP #26
SLOW IT DOWN
(EVEN SLOWER THAN YOU THINK)

When we learn how to do something new, our immediate urge is to do it again, faster. This is known as the Hey, Look at Me! reflex. This urge for speed makes perfect sense, but it can also create sloppiness, particularly when it comes to hard skills (see Tip #8). We trade precision—and long-term performance—for a temporary thrill. So, slow it down.

Super-slow practice works like a magnifying glass: It lets us sense our errors more clearly, and thus fix them. Slow practice is used by many talent hotbeds to teach hard skills, from the Spartak Tennis Club (where students swing in such slow motion they resemble ballet dancers) to the Septien School of Contemporary Music (where performers learn a new song by singing one slow note at a time). Ben Hogan, considered to have perhaps the most technically sound golf swing in the history of the game, routinely practiced so slowly that when he finally contacted the ball, it moved about an inch. As the saying goes, "It's not how fast you can do it. It's how slowly you can do it correctly."

TIP #27

CLOSE YOUR EYES

One of the quickest ways to deepen practice is also one of the simplest: Close your eyes. Musicians have long used this technique to improve feel and accuracy, but it also works for other skills. Michael Jordan practiced free throws with his eyes shut; Navy SEAL training includes generous helpings of pitch-black darkness during which soldiers learn to disassemble and reassemble their weapons, and, in one exercise, cooperate to pitch a tent; yoga and martial-arts practitioners frequently close their eyes to improve body awareness and balance.

The reason, in each case, is the same. Closing your eyes is a swift way to nudge you to the edges of your ability, to get you into your sweet spot. It sweeps away distraction and engages your other senses to provide new feedback. It helps you engrave the blueprint of a task on your brain by making even a familiar skill seem strange and fresh.

TIP #28
MIME IT

At talent hotbeds you will see people swinging golf clubs and tennis rackets at empty air, playing the piano on tabletops, and skiing imaginary slalom courses with their feet fixed on the floor. It looks crazy, but from a deep-practice perspective it makes sense. Removing everything except the essential action lets you focus on what matters most: making the right reach.

TIP #29

WHEN YOU GET IT RIGHT, MARK THE SPOT

One of the most fulfilling moments of a practice session is when you have your first perfect rep. When this happens, freeze. Rewind the mental tape and play the move again in your mind. Memorize the feeling, the rhythm, the physical and mental sensations. The point is to mark this moment—*this* is the spot where you want to go again and again. This is not the finish—it's the new starting line for perfecting the skill until it becomes automatic. As Kimberly Meier-Sims of the Sato Center for Suzuki Studies says, "Practice *begins* when you get it right."

TIP #30
TAKE A NAP

This is one of my favorite tips. Napping is common in talent hotbeds, and features both anecdotal and scientific justification.

The anecdotal: Albert Einstein was good at physics, and he was really good at his daily post-lunch twenty-minute snooze. Other famous nappers include Leonardo da Vinci, Napoleon Bonaparte, Winston Churchill, Thomas Edison, Ronald Reagan, John F. Kennedy, and John D. Rockefeller. Spend time with any professional athletic team, and you'll find that they're also professional nappers.

The science: Napping is good for the learning brain, because it helps strengthen the connections formed during practice and prepare the brain for the next session. Researchers at the University of California, Berkeley, found that napping for ninety minutes improved memory scores by 10 percent, while skipping a nap made them decline by 10 percent. "You need sleep before learning, to prepare your brain, like a dry sponge, to absorb new information," said the study's lead investigator, Dr. Matthew Walker.

TIP #31

TO LEARN A NEW MOVE, EXAGGERATE IT

Think of the way parents teach their babies new words—they stretch out each sound, overemphasize it, overdo it. There's a good reason for this. Going too far helps us understand where the boundaries are.

To learn a new move, exaggerate it. If the move calls for you to lift your knees, lift them to the ceiling. If it calls for you to press hard on the guitar strings, press with all your might. If it calls for you to emphasize a point while speaking in public, emphasize with theatricality. Don't be halfhearted. You can always dial back later. Go too far so you can feel the outer edges of the move, and then work on building the skill with precision.

TIP #32
MAKE POSITIVE REACHES

There's a moment just before every rep when you are faced with a choice: You can either focus your attention on the target (what you want to do) or you can focus on the possible mistake (what you want to avoid). This tip is simple: Always focus on the positive move, not the negative one.

For example, a golfer lining up a putt should tell herself, "Center the stroke," not "Don't pull this putt to the left." A violinist faced with a difficult passage should tell himself, "Nail that A-flat," not "Oh boy, I hope I don't miss that A-flat." Psychologists call this "positive framing," and provide plentiful theories of how framing affects our subconscious mind. The point is, it always works better to reach for what you want to accomplish, not away from what you want to avoid.

TIP #33
TO LEARN FROM A BOOK,
CLOSE THE BOOK

Let's pretend that one week from now you will take a test on the next ten pages of this book. You have thirty minutes to study. Which practice method would help you get a better grade?

A) Reading those ten pages four times in a row, and trying to memorize them.
B) Reading those ten pages once, then closing the book and writing a one-page summary.

It's not even close. Research shows that people who follow strategy B remember 50 percent more material over the long term than people who follow strategy A. This is because of one of deep practice's most fundamental rules: *Learning is reaching*. Passively reading a book—a relatively effortless process, letting the words wash over you like a warm bath—doesn't put you in the sweet spot. Less reaching equals less learning.

On the other hand, closing the book and writing a summary forces you to figure out the key points (one set of reaches), process and organize those ideas so they make sense (more reaches), and write them on the page (still more reaches, along with repetition). The equation is always the same: More reaching equals more learning.

TIP #34
USE THE SANDWICH TECHNIQUE

Deep practice is about finding and fixing mistakes, so the question naturally pops up: What's the best way to make sure you don't repeat mistakes? One way is to employ the sandwich technique. It goes like this:

1. Make the correct move.
2. Make the incorrect move.
3. Make the correct move again.

The goal is to reinforce the correct move and to put a spotlight on the mistake, preventing it from slipping past undetected and becoming wired into your circuitry.

TIP #35
USE THE 3 X 10 TECHNIQUE

This piece of advice comes from Dr. Douglas Fields, a neurologist at the National Institutes of Health in Bethesda, Maryland, who researches memory and learning. He discovered that our brains make stronger connections when they're stimulated three times with a rest period of ten minutes between each stimulation. The real-world translation: To learn something most effectively, practice it three times, with ten-minute breaks between each rep. "I apply this to learning all the time in my own life, and it works," Fields says. "For example, in mastering a difficult piece of music on the guitar, I practice, then I do something else for ten minutes, then I practice again [and so on]."

TIP #36
INVENT DAILY TESTS

Daily routine in the talent hotbeds is full of little tests. The tests aren't scientific, and they're not treated as verdicts—they're far more like targeted workouts, invented by the performers and their teachers.

For example, Tiger Woods has created a test in which he has to hit a certain percentage of shots inside a certain distance each day (80 percent of eight-irons within twenty feet, for example). At Meadowmount, the music school, teachers will provide an impromptu test by tucking a five-dollar bill inside a student's cello or violin—if he plays the song perfectly, he wins the money. Robert Lansdorp, the coach of former tennis champions Pete Sampras, Tracy Austin, and Lindsay Davenport, uses a similar game with ten-dollar bills tucked inside small orange cones—hit the cone, win the money. Teachers don't see this as a bribe, incidentally, but as a bit of motivational juice to add interest. As the cello teacher Hans Jensen explained to me, "The important thing, the only thing, is to help the student push themselves. There are many ways to do that; whether it's money or chocolate or pride or something else doesn't really matter."

To invent a good test, ask yourself: What's one key element of this skill? How can I isolate my accuracy or reliability, and measure it? How can I make it fun, quick, and repeatable, so I can track my progress?

TIP #37

TO CHOOSE THE BEST PRACTICE METHOD, USE THE R.E.P.S. GAUGE

The biggest problem in choosing a practice strategy is not that there are too few options, but that there are too many. How do you identify the best methods? This tip provides a way to measure practice effectiveness. It's called the R.E.P.S. gauge. Each letter stands for a key element of deep practice.

R: Reaching and Repeating
E: Engagement
P: Purposefulness
S: Strong, Speedy Feedback.

ELEMENT 1: REACHING AND REPEATING. Does the practice have you operating on the edge of your ability, reaching and repeating?

Scenario: two math teachers teaching the multiplication tables to thirty students.

- Teacher A selects a single student to write the tables on the board.
- Teacher B creates a "game show" format in which a multiplication problem is posed verbally to the entire class, then a single student is called on to answer.

Result: Teacher B chose the better option because it creates thirty reaches per question. In Classroom A, only one student has to reach—everybody else can lean back and observe. In Classroom B, however, *every single member of the class* has to reach in case their name is called.

ELEMENT 2: ENGAGEMENT. Is the practice immersive? Does it command your attention? Does it use emotion to propel you toward a goal?

Scenario: two trumpet students trying to learn a short, tough passage in a song.

- Trumpeter A plays the passage twenty times.
- Trumpeter B tries to play the passage perfectly—with zero mistakes—five times in a row. If she makes any mistake, the count goes back to zero and she starts over.

Result: Student B made the better choice, because the method is more engaging. Playing a passage twenty times in a row is boring, a chore where you're simply counting the reps until you're done. But playing five times perfectly, when any mistake sends you back to zero, is intensively engaging.

ELEMENT 3: PURPOSEFULNESS. Does the task directly connect to the skill you want to build?

Scenario: Two basketball teams keep losing games because of missed free throws.

- Team A practices free throws at the end of a practice, with each player shooting fifty free throws alone.
- Team B practices free throws intermittently during a full-court scrimmage, with the fouled player shooting while tired and under pressure, as in a game.

Result: Team B made the better choice, because their practice connects to the skill they want to build, the ability to make free throws under pressure, while exhausted. (No player ever gets to shoot fifty straight in a game.)

ELEMENT 4: STRONG, SPEEDY FEEDBACK. Does the learner receive a stream of accurate information about his performance—where he succeeded and where he made mistakes?

Scenario: two high school students trying to improve their SAT scores.

- Student A spends a Saturday taking a mock version of the SAT test, then receives the test results one week later.
- Student B spends a Saturday taking a mini version of each section, grading herself and reviewing each test in detail as soon as it's completed.

Result: Student B made the better choice, because the feedback is direct and immediate. Learning swiftly where she went wrong (and where she went right) will tend to stick, while finding out a week later will have little effect.

The idea of this gauge is simple: When given a choice between two practice methods, or when you're inventing a new test or game, pick the one that maximizes these four qualities, the one with the most R.E.P.S. The larger lesson here is to pay attention to the design of your practice. Small changes in method can create large increases in learning velocity.

TIP #38
STOP BEFORE YOU'RE EXHAUSTED

In many skills, particularly athletic, medical, and military ones, there's a long tradition of working until total exhaustion. This tradition has its uses, particularly for improving fitness and mental toughness, and for forging emotional connections within a group.

But when it comes to learning, the science is clear: Exhaustion is the enemy. Fatigue slows brains. It triggers errors, lessens concentration, and leads to shortcuts that create bad habits. It's no coincidence that most talent hotbeds put a premium on practicing when people are fresh, usually in the morning, if possible. When exhaustion creeps in, it's time to quit.

TIP #39
PRACTICE IMMEDIATELY AFTER PERFORMANCE

The previous tip was about the importance of practicing when you're fresh. This tip is about a different kind of freshness, which comes in the moment just after a performance, game, or competition. At that moment, practicing is probably the last thing you want to do. But it's the first thing you should do, if you're not too worn out, because it helps you target your weak points and fix them. As the golfer Jack Nicklaus said, "I always achieve my most productive practice after an actual round. Then, the mistakes are fresh in my mind and I can go to the practice tee and work specifically on those mistakes."

TIP #40
JUST BEFORE SLEEP,
WATCH A MENTAL MOVIE

This is a useful habit I've heard about from dozens of top performers, ranging from surgeons to athletes to comedians. Just before falling asleep, they play a movie of their idealized performance in their heads. A wide body of research supports this idea, linking visualization to improved performance, motivation, mental toughness, and confidence. Treat it as a way to rev the engine of your unconscious mind, so it spends more time churning toward your goals.

TIP #41
END ON A POSITIVE NOTE

A practice session should end like a good meal—with a small, sweet reward. It could be playing a favorite game or it could be more literal. (Chocolate works quite well.) My ten-year-old daughter ends her violin practices with a foot-stomping rendition of the bluegrass tune "Old Joe Clark."

TIP #42

SIX WAYS TO BE A BETTER
TEACHER OR COACH

Sooner or later, no matter who you are, you'll find yourself being a teacher, a coach, or a mentor. It might happen at home, at work, or on the playing field, but when it happens, it helps to have a few basic skills. Here, from the master coaches I've researched, are six pieces of advice.

1) Use the First Few Seconds to Connect on an Emotional Level

Take a moment and recall the best teacher, coach, or mentor you've ever known. If you're like most people, your memories are less about what that person did than about the way that person made you *feel*. You knew, somehow, that they saw something special in you, and understood you. You trusted them.

Effective teaching is built on trust, and when it comes to trust, we humans are consistent: We decide if we're going to trust someone in the first few seconds of the interaction. This is why good teachers use the first few seconds to connect on an emotional level, especially on the first encounter. There are lots of tools for making this connection—eye contact, body language, empathy, and humor being some of the most effective—but whatever you use, make sure you prioritize that connection above all else. Before you can teach, you have to show that you care.

2) Avoid Giving Long Speeches—Instead, Deliver Vivid Chunks of Information

Thanks to movies, many of us grow up thinking that great teachers and coaches stand nobly in front of groups and deliver inspiring speeches. Nothing could be further from the truth. Master teachers and coaches don't stand in front; they stand alongside the individuals they're helping. They don't give long speeches; they deliver useful information in small, vivid chunks.

As a Little League coach, I was accustomed to giving instruction to an entire team at the same time; for example, teaching them all the proper technique to field a grounder. But after spending time with master coaches, I started focusing on delivering short, targeted, customized messages to each player, one at a time. And it worked a lot better. Not only did players catch on more quickly, but the process also forged closer bonds of communication.

When you're coaching, picture the person's brain lighting up, the wires sparking fitfully, reaching to make new connections. The question is not what big important message you can deliver. The question is, what vivid, concise message can you deliver right now that will guide her toward making the right reach?

3) Be Allergic to Mushy Language

One of the most common mistakes teachers and coaches make is using mushy, imprecise language. For example, when a Little League coach tells a batter to "move the hands higher." How high should the hands move? To the shoulders? Above the head?

To avoid this, use language that is concrete and specific. For example:

- "Move your hands higher" is vague. "Move your hands next to your ear" is concrete.
- "Play the song a little faster" is vague. "Match the metronome" is concrete.
- "Please work more closely with the sales team" is vague. "Please check in with the sales team for ten minutes every morning" is concrete.

All good teaching follows the same blueprint: Try *this concrete thing*. Now try *this concrete thing*. Now try combining them into *this concrete thing*. Communicate with precise nouns and numbers—things you can see and touch and measure—and avoid adjectives and adverbs, which don't tell you precisely what to do.

4) Make a Scorecard for Learning

Life is full of scorecards: sales figures, performance rankings, test scores, tournament results. The problem with those scorecards is that they can distort priorities, bending us toward short-term outcomes and away from the learning process. We've all seen it happen, in business and in sports. Organizations that focus maniacally on winning today tend to lose sight of the larger goal: learning and developing competencies for the long run.

The solution is to create your own scorecard. Pick a metric that measures the skill you want to develop, and start keeping track of it. Use that measure to motivate and orient your learners. As a saying goes, "You are what you count."

For example, I've encountered a number of top soccer, basketball, and hockey coaches who track the number of smart passes their team makes during a game, and who use this number—not the score—as the most accurate measure of their team's success. The players catch on, and try to exceed themselves each game. Regardless of what happens on the scoreboard, this number gives them an accurate way to measure their real progress.

Tony Hsieh (pronounced "Shay"), a founder of the online shoe retailer Zappos, started out with the desire to create the most skilled customer-service team in the world. The usual scorecard of customer-service success is customers served per hour. But for Hsieh, that scorecard made no sense. He didn't want to be merely efficient—he wanted to make people happy. So Zappos ignored the usual scorecard and began tracking the occasions when their customer-service representatives went above and beyond the call of duty—"delivering wow," in Zappos parlance. Those moments, tallied and celebrated by the company, form the scorecard. And it seems to work: On a dare, Hsieh once phoned Zappos anonymously in the middle of the night and asked if he could order a pizza. He shortly received a list of the five pizza places closest to his location that were still open.

5) Maximize "Reachfulness"

Reachfulness is the essence of learning. It happens when the learner is leaning forward, stretching, struggling, and improving. The point of this rule is that good teachers/coaches/mentors find ways to design environments that tip people away from passivity and toward reachful action. This is why good sports coaches will avoid activities where players stand in lines, waiting their turn, and instead employ lots of small, intense games. But the idea of reachfulness applies to more than sports.

Recently, United Parcel Service was struggling with its driver-training program. Retention was down; injury and dissatisfaction were up. UPS responded with a novel program: It canceled classroom lectures and built a $34-million training center that resembled a small town, so the trainees could learn by doing. The trainees didn't hear lectures about how to drive, stack, or deliver—they actually did it. To teach balance, UPS trainers secretly squirted soap on the floor and had trainees walk across it carrying a load of boxes. (The trainees were hooked up to safety harnesses, so they weren't injured.) The program was a success; retention, performance, and satisfaction are up.

Some progressive schools increase reachfulness through a technique called "flipping the classroom." The term refers to changing the traditional model, in which students spend class time listening to a lecture and then do reinforcement work at home. In a flipped classroom, students do the reverse. They listen to lectures at home, online, and spend class time actively struggling with the work: doing problems, wrestling with concepts—in essence, reaching—while the teacher walks around, coach-style, and helps individuals one at a time. In a yearlong study of algebra students at one

California high school, the flipped classroom scored 23 percent higher on tests than the conventional classroom.

The larger point is that being a good teacher means thinking like a designer. Ask yourself: What kind of space will create the most reachful environment? How can you replace moments of passivity with moments of active learning?

6) Aim to Create Independent Learners

Your long-term goal as a teacher, coach, or mentor is to help your learners improve so much that they no longer need you. To do this, avoid becoming the center of attention. Aim instead to create an environment where people can keep reaching on their own. Whenever possible, step away and create moments of independence. Think of your job as building a little master-coach chip in their brains—a tiny version of you, guiding them as they go forward.

SUSTAINING PROGRESS

Embrace Repetition, Cultivate Grit,
and Keep Big Goals Secret

Developing talent is like taking a cross-country hike. You will encounter challenges; you will hit snags, plateaus, and steep paths; motivation will ebb and flow. To sustain progress, it's necessary to be flexible one moment and stubborn the next, to deal with immediate obstacles while staying focused on the horizon: in short, to be a resourceful traveler. The tips in this section are meant to give you a few tools for the journey.

TIP #43
EMBRACE REPETITION

Repetition has a bad reputation. We tend to think of it as dull and uninspiring. But this perception is titanically wrong. Repetition is the single most powerful lever we have to improve our skills, because it uses the built-in mechanism for making the wires of our brains faster and more accurate (see the Appendix, page 117).

When U.S. Navy SEAL Team 6 mounted its May 2011 raid on Osama bin Laden's compound in Pakistan, it prepared by constructing full-scale replicas of the compound in North Carolina and Nevada, and rehearsing for three weeks. Dozens of times the SEALs simulated the operation. Dozens of times, they created various conditions they might encounter. They used the power of repetition to build the circuitry needed for the job.

Another example: Moe Norman was a shy Canadian who played briefly on the professional golf tour in the 1960s and '70s. He was also, in most estimations, the most accurate golfer in history. Norman shot seventeen holes in one, three scores of 59, and, in Tiger Woods's estimation, ranked as one of two golfers in history who "owned their swing" (the other was Ben Hogan). Norman was also a likely autistic who, at a young age, became enraptured by the power of repetition. From the age of sixteen onward, Norman hit eight hundred to a thousand balls a day, five days a week; calluses grew so thick on his hands he had to pare them with a knife. Because of his emotional struggles, Norman had difficulty competing in tournaments. But at a demonstration in 1995, he hit fifteen hundred drives in a row, all of them landing within fifteen yards of each other. As Woods put it, Norman "woke up every day and knew he was going to hit it well. Every day. It's frightening how straight he hits it."

Embracing repetition means changing your mindset; instead of viewing it as a chore, view it as your most powerful tool. As the martial artist and actor Bruce Lee said, "I fear not the man who has practiced ten thousand kicks once, but I fear the man who has practiced one kick ten thousand times."

TIP #44
HAVE A BLUE-COLLAR MIND-SET

From a distance, top performers seem to live charmed, cushy lives. When you look closer, however, you'll find that they spend vast portions of their life intensively practicing their craft. Their mind-set is not entitled or arrogant; it's 100-percent blue collar: They get up in the morning and go to work every day, whether they feel like it or not.

As the artist Chuck Close says, "Inspiration is for amateurs."

TIP #45

FOR EVERY HOUR OF COMPETITION, SPEND FIVE HOURS PRACTICING

Games are fun. Tournaments are exciting. Contests are thrilling. They also slow skill development, for four reasons:

1. The presence of other people diminishes an appetite for risks, nudging you away from the sweet spot.
2. Games reduce the number of quality reps.
3. The pressure of games distorts priorities, encouraging shortcuts in technique.
4. Games encourage players, coaches, and parents to judge success by the scoreboard rather than by how much was learned.

At Spartak, the tennis club in Moscow, coaches enforce a simple rule: Young players must practice for three years before entering competitive tournaments. (See Tip #10.) While I can't imagine that such a rule would fly in America, it reflects Spartak's determination to build trusty, reliable forehands and backhands before injecting the distorting pressures of competition.

Don't get me wrong. Public competition is a great thing. It teaches invaluable lessons about teamwork, it helps build emotional control, and it's fun. But it's also, in many cases, a deeply inefficient way to improve skill. One solution to the problem is to make public performance a special occasion, not a routine. A five-to-one ratio of practice time to performance time is a good starting point; ten to one is even better.

TIP #46
DON'T WASTE TIME TRYING TO BREAK BAD HABITS—INSTEAD, BUILD NEW ONES

When it comes to dealing with bad habits, many of us try to attack the problem head-on, by trying to break the habit. This tactic, of course, doesn't work, and we're left with the old truth—habits are tough to break. The blame lies with our brains. While they are really good at building circuits, they are awful at unbuilding them. Try as you might to break it, the bad habit is still up there, wired into your brain, waiting patiently for a chance to be used.

The solution is to ignore the bad habit and put your energy toward building a new habit that will override the old one. A good example of this technique is found in the work of the Shyness Clinic, a program based in Los Altos, California, that helps chronically shy people improve their social skills. The clinic's therapists don't delve into a client's personal history; they don't try to "fix" anything. Instead, they focus on building new skills through what they call a social fitness model: a series of simple, intense, gradually escalating workouts that develop new social muscles. One of the first workouts for a Shyness Clinic client is to walk up to a stranger and ask for the time. Each day the workout grows more strenuous—soon clients are asking five strangers for the time, making phone calls to acquaintances, or chatting with a stranger in an elevator. After a few months, some clients are "socially fit" enough to perform the ultimate workout: They walk into a crowded grocery store, lift a watermelon above their head, and purposely drop it on the floor, triumphantly enduring the stares of dozens of strangers. (The grocery store cleanup crew doesn't enjoy this quite as much as the clients do.)

To build new habits, start slowly. Expect to feel stupid and clumsy and frustrated at first—after all, the new wires haven't been built yet, and your brain still wants to follow the old pattern. Build the new habit by gradually increasing the difficulty, little by little. It takes time, but it's the only way new habits grow. For more insights on this process, read *The Power of Habit,* by Charles Duhigg.

TIP #47

TO LEARN IT MORE DEEPLY, TEACH IT

We instinctively tend to separate learners into groups based on skill and age—the twelve-year-olds over here, the thirteen-year-olds over there. Many talent hotbeds, however, use an open floor plan, where groups of various ages are mingled so they can watch, teach, and learn from each other. I saw a baseball practice on Frank Curiel Field in Curaçao that featured ninety kids, aged seven to sixteen. Each older player was paired off with a younger player, teaching them how to bat, throw, and catch. I also saw this dynamic at several successful Montessori* schools I visited, where classes were intermin-

* A method of schooling founded by the Italian educator Maria Montessori that emphasizes collaborative, explorative learning, and whose alumni include Google's founders, Sergey Brin and Larry Page; Wikipedia founder Jimmy Wales; video-game designer Will Wright; Amazon's founder, Jeff Bezos; chef Julia Child; and rap impresario Sean Combs.

gled to create this same dynamic: The older kids teach the younger ones.

This works because when you communicate a skill to someone, you come to understand it more deeply yourself. Mixed-age groups also provide younger children vivid models to stare at (see Tip #1), and nourish empathy in older children. When you see someone struggle, and help them through it, you improve your ability to deal with your own struggles. The saying "Those who can't do, teach" should be rewritten as "Doers who teach do better."

TIP #48
GIVE A NEW SKILL A MINIMUM OF EIGHT WEEKS

When it comes to growing new skills, eight weeks seems to be an important threshold. It's the length of many top-level training programs around the world, from the Navy SEALs' physical-conditioning program to the Meadowmount School of Music program to the clinics of the Bolshoi Ballet to the mission training for the Mercury astronauts. A recent study at Massachusetts General Hospital showed that practicing meditation for twenty-seven minutes a day created lasting brain changes in (you guessed it) eight weeks.

Of course, this doesn't mean that you can be proficient in any skill in eight weeks. Rather, it underlines two more basic points: 1) Constructing and honing neural circuitry takes time, no matter who you are; and

2) Resilience and grit are vital tools, particularly in the early phases of learning. Don't make judgments too early. Keep at it, even if you don't feel immediate improvement. Give your talent (that is, your brain) the time it needs to grow.

TIP #49

WHEN YOU GET STUCK, MAKE A SHIFT

We all know the feeling. You start out in a new skill, you progress swiftly for a while, and then all of a sudden . . . you stop. Those are called plateaus. I hit one recently, in fact, after our family bought a Ping-Pong table. For a few months, I improved each time I played. Then, suddenly, the progress stopped. This was a problem, because my teenage son, who hadn't hit his plateau, started thumping me. The scores went from being fairly even to 21–10, 21–8. What happened?

A plateau happens when your brain achieves a level of automaticity; in other words, when you can perform a skill on autopilot, without conscious thought. Our brains love autopilot, because in most situations it's pretty handy. It lets us chew gum and walk and ride bikes without having to think about it, freeing our brains for more important tasks. When it comes to developing talent, however, autopilot is the enemy, because it creates plateaus.

Research by Dr. K. Anders Ericsson, a professor of psychology at Florida State University and coeditor of *The Cambridge Handbook of Expertise and Expert Performance,* shows that the best way past a plateau is to jostle yourself beyond it; to change your practice method so you disrupt your autopilot and rebuild a faster, better circuit. One way to do this is to speed things up—to force yourself to do the task faster than you normally would. Or you can slow things down—going so slowly that you highlight previously undetected mistakes. Or you can do the task in reverse order, turn it inside out or upside down. It doesn't matter which technique you use, as long as you find a way to knock yourself out of autopilot and into your sweet spot.

In my case, it turned out that one half of our Ping-Pong table could be raised into a vertical position, creating a practice wall. I started hitting against the wall a few minutes a day. At first it felt awkward and wrong— the ball, rebounding from a few feet closer than I was accustomed to, shot back at me so quickly that I could barely get a paddle on it. But I got used to it, gradually adjusting to the faster pace. The games with my son got a lot more competitive; I even started winning a few.

TIP #50
CULTIVATE YOUR GRIT

Grit is that mix of passion, perseverance, and self-discipline that keeps us moving forward in spite of obstacles. It's not flashy, and that's precisely the point. In a world in which we're frequently distracted by sparkly displays of skill, grit makes the difference in the long run.

Recently, a University of Pennsylvania researcher named Angela Duckworth measured the influence of grit on twelve hundred first-year West Point cadets before they began a brutal summer training course called the Beast Barracks. Before the course began, she gave the cadets a brief test: seventeen questions that asked them to rate their own ability to stick to goals, to be motivated by failure, and to persist in the face of obstacles. It turned out that this test—which took about two minutes to complete—was uncannily accurate at predicting whether or not a cadet succeeded, far exceeding West Point's complex set of predictive criteria, including IQ, psychological test results, grade-point average, and physical fitness. The grit test has since been used to predict success in schools, business, and a variety of other settings.

Grit isn't inborn. It's developed, like a muscle, and that development starts with awareness. To take Duckworth's test, do a computer search for "Grit Survey" (or go directly to www.authentichappiness.sas.upenn.edu/tests/SameAnswers/t.aspx?id=1246). Take the test and use your score as a way to reflect on the role of this quality in your life. For instance, when you hit an obstacle, how do you react? Do you tend to focus on a long-term goal, or move from interest to interest? What are you seeking in the long run? Begin to pay attention to places in your life where you've got grit, and celebrate them in yourself and others.

TIP #51
KEEP YOUR BIG GOALS SECRET

While it's natural and oh so tempting to want to announce big goals, it's smarter to keep them to yourself. In a 2009 experiment at New York University, 163 subjects were given a difficult work project and forty-five minutes to spend on it. Half the subjects were told to announce their goals, while half were told to keep quiet. The subjects who announced their goals quit after only an average of thirty-three minutes, and reported feeling satisfied with their work. Those who kept their mouths shut, however, worked the entire forty-five minutes, and remained strongly motivated. (In fact, when the experiment ended, they wanted to keep working.)

Telling others about your big goals makes them less likely to happen, because it creates an unconscious payoff—tricking our brains into thinking we've already accomplished the goal. Keeping our big goals to ourselves is one of the smartest goals we can set.

TIP #52
"THINK LIKE A GARDENER,
WORK LIKE A CARPENTER"

We all want to improve our skills quickly—today, if not sooner. But the truth is, talent grows slowly. You would not criticize a seedling because it was not yet a tall oak tree; nor should you get upset because your skill circuitry is in the growth stage. Instead, build it with daily deep practice.

To do this, it helps to "think like a gardener and work like a carpenter." I heard this saying at Spartak. Think patiently, without judgment. Work steadily, strategically, knowing that each piece connects to a larger whole.

GLOSSARY

Deep practice (*n*), also called deliberate practice: The form of learning marked by 1) the willingness to operate on the edge of your ability, aiming for targets that are just out of reach, and 2) the embrace of attentive repetition.

Ignition (*n*): The motivational process that occurs when your identity becomes linked to a long-term vision of your future. Triggers significant amounts of unconscious energy; usually marked by the realization *That is who I want to be.*

Reach (*v*): The act of stretching slightly beyond your current abilities toward a target, which causes the brain to form new connections. Reaching invariably creates mistakes, which are the guideposts you use to improve the next attempt.

Rep (*n*, abbreviation for *repetition*): The act of attentively repeating an action, often with slight variances at gradually increasing difficulty, which causes the brain's pathways to increase speed and improve accuracy.

Rule of Ten Thousand Hours (*n*): The scientific finding that all world-class experts in every field have spent a minimum of ten thousand hours intensively practicing their craft. While this number is sometimes misinterpreted as a magical threshold, in reality it functions as a rule of thumb underlining a larger truth: Greatness is not born, but grown through deep practice, no matter who you are.

Shallow practice (*n*): The opposite of deep practice, marked by lack of intensity, vagueness of goal, and/ or the unwillingness to reach beyond current abilities. Often caused by an aversion to making mistakes; results in vastly slowed skill acquisition and learning.

Sweet spot (*n*): The zone on the edge of current ability where learning happens fastest. Marked by a frequency of mistakes, and also by the recognition of those mistakes (see Tip #13).

THE NEW SCIENCE OF TALENT DEVELOPMENT
A BRIEF LOOK AT MYELIN

Much of the new research about talent revolves around the brain, specifically a substance called myelin. Here's what you need to know.

Myelin is an insulator (you might recall the term "myelin sheath" from biology class). This refers to its function of wrapping the wires of our brain in exactly the same way that electrical tape wraps around an electrical wire: It makes the signal move faster and prevents it from leaking out. For the past hundred years or so, scientists considered myelin and its associated cells to be inert. After all, it looked like insulation, and it didn't appear to react to anything.

Except the early scientists were wrong. It turns out that myelin does react—it grows in response to electrical activity, i.e., practice. In fact, studies show that myelin grows in proportion to the hours spent in practice. It's a simple system, and can be thought of this way: Every time you perform a rep, your brain adds another layer of myelin to those particular wires. The more you practice, the more layers of myelin you earn, the more quickly and accurately the signal travels, and the more skill you acquire.

"What do good athletes do when they train?" asks Dr. George Bartzokis, a professor of neurology at UCLA. "They send precise impulses along wires that give the signal to myelinate that wire. They end up, after all the training, with a super-duper wire—lots of bandwidth, a high-speed T-3 line. That's what makes them different than the rest of us."

A few other facts worth knowing:

- Action is vital. Myelin doesn't grow when you think about practicing. It grows when you actually practice—when you send electricity through your wires.
- Myelin wraps—it doesn't unwrap. Like a highway paving machine, myelination happens in one direction. Once a skill circuit is insulated, you can't uninsulate it (except through age or disease). This is why habits are tough to break (see Tip #46).
- You can add myelin throughout life. It arrives in

a series of waves throughout childhood, creating critical learning periods. The net amount of myelin peaks around age fifty, but the myelin machinery keeps functioning into old age, which is why we can keep learning new things no matter what our age.

Studies have linked practice to myelin growth and improved performance in such diverse skills as reading, vocabulary, music, and sports. The research is still in its early phases, but it is threatening to rewrite the old saying. Practice doesn't make perfect. Practice makes myelin, and myelin makes perfect.

For more information, read *The Talent Code*.

FURTHER READING

The Rare Find, by George Anders
Willpower, by Roy F. Baumeister and John Tierney
Developing Talent in Young People, by Benjamin Bloom
The Social Animal, by David Brooks
Talent is Overrated, by Geoff Colvin
The Power of Habit, by Charles Duhigg
The Brain that Changes Itself, by Norman Doidge
Mindset, by Carol S. Dweck
The Road to Excellence, edited by K. Anders Ericsson
Outliers, by Malcolm Gladwell
Switch, by Chip Heath and Dan Heath
Steal Like an Artist, by Austin Kleon
Brain Rules, by John Medina
You Haven't Taught Until They Have Learned, by Swen
    Nater and Ronald Gallimore

Intelligence and How to Get It, by Richard E. Nisbett
Drive, by Daniel H. Pink
Being Wrong, by Kathryn Schultz
The Genius in All of Us, by David Shenk
Bounce, by Matthew Syed

ACKNOWLEDGMENTS

I would like to thank the community of teachers, coaches, readers, and friends who contributed their ideas to this book, including Dr. George Bartzokis, Dr. Robert A. Bjork, Bob Bowman, Cindy Bristow, Marco Cardinale, Jenny Conner, Chris Chard, Dr. Paul Cox, Marg Daigneault, Bill Dorenkott, Anson Dorrance, Dr. R. Douglas Fields, Chris Frank, Michael Fumagalli, Richie Graham, Hans Jensen, Renita Kalhorn, John Kessel, Dale Kirby, Tom Martinez, Kimberly Meier-Sims, Tom Peters, Jamie Posnanski, Rod Roth, Mari Sato, Linda Septien, Daniel Silver, Stephen Sims, Richard Stanbaugh, Dr. Gio Valiante, and Dr. Peter F. Vint.

Thanks also to Mike Rohde for his illustrations, to Kate Norris for her copy editing, to David Black for being my brilliant agent for the last two decades, and to my terrifically talented editor, Andy Ward, for his vision and friendship. Thanks to my brothers, Maurice and Jon, for their insightful help and guidance, and to my parents for their support and love. Thanks most to my wonderful kids, Aidan, Katie, Lia, and Zoe, and to my wife, Jen, who makes all good things possible.

ABOUT THE AUTHOR

DANIEL COYLE is the author of *The Talent Code, Hardball: A Season in the Projects,* and the *New York Times* bestseller *Lance Armstrong's War,* and is a contributing editor for *Outside* magazine. He divides his time between Cleveland, Ohio, and Homer, Alaska, with his wife, Jen, and their four children.

NOTES

NOTES

NOTES

NOTES

NOTES

NOTES

_____

_____

_____

_____

_____

_____

_____

_____

_____

_____

_____

_____

_____

_____

_____

_____

_____

NOTES

NOTES

NOTES

NOTES